The Autism
Social Skills Picture Book
Teaching Communication, Play and Emotion

By Jed Baker, Ph.D.

Future Horizons, Inc.

All marketing and publishing rights guaranteed to and reserved by

Future Horizons, Inc.
721 W. Abram Street
Arlington, TX 76013

800.489.0727 Toll Free
817.277.0727
817.277.2270 Fax

www.FutureHorizons-autism.com
email: info@FutureHorizons-autism.com

ISBN   1-885477-91-0

Dedication

This book is dedicated to the countless students and parents who have taught us what to teach and how to make it comprehensible. To best thank them, a portion of all proceeds from the book will return to programming for the students at the Valley Program in Northern Valley Regional High School Districts.

Acknowledgment

I wish to thank all the children and their families who participated in the creation of the pictures for this book. I must acknowledge two individuals in particular at Northern Valley Regional High School Districts. First is John McKeon, Special Education Director, who lent his unwavering support and encouragement for all creative projects that might help his students. Secondly, Ellen Doyle, Behavioral Consultant, really sparked this project by first suggesting the need for more visually based learning tools for her students.

Veronica Palmer, my editor, must also be mentioned, as her help was crucial to systematize and clarify the pictures and accompanying text.

Finally, my wife Beth and our children, Jake and Lindsay, constantly remind me of the paramount importance of humor and fun in everything you do, especially teaching.

■ ■ Contents ■ ■

■ PART TWO - SOCIAL SKILL PICTURE STORIES

PART ONE

THE NATURE OF AUTISM

A Brief Look at Autism

Autism is a term used to describe a wide range of symptoms that span across an individual's sensory, cognitive, motor, language, and social-emotional development. Current diagnostic criteria characterize autism as involving deficits in three general areas: (a) social interaction, (b) communication, and (c) repetitive and ritualistic behaviors (American Psychiatric Association, 1994).

Problems with social interaction can include difficulties initiating or responding to communication or play, difficulties using or responding to non-verbal gestures (e.g., pointing out objects), lack of or inconsistent eye contact, impairments in responding to others' feelings, and subsequent failure to develop peer relationships. Understanding what to do or say in social situations is a core problem for autistic individuals.

Communication problems may include pragmatic, semantic, and structural language difficulties. Pragmatic language refers to the social use of language, as is involved in sustaining or initiating communication. For example, some autistic individuals may appear to have perfectly intact language in terms of their ability to express themselves and understand others, yet they may have great trouble with social communication, talking at people instead of with people, relaying factual information or phrases memorized from TV shows without responding to what their listener is saying or doing. Many autistic individuals also have a semantic language problem involving trouble understanding the meaning of words, especially with abstract words, metaphors, or sayings. For example, they may hear the saying, "Don't let the cat out of the bag" and search for a cat and bag rather than grasp the symbolic meaning regarding not spoiling a surprise. Structural language problems refer to difficulties with the use of grammar and syntax. Many autistic individuals may have difficulty putting sentences together and understanding grammatically correct sentence structure.

Repetitive and ritualistic behaviors reflect a preference for sameness and repetition with regards to interests, daily routine, and body movements. Many youngsters with autism develop a fascination with a particular area of interest and elaborate on that interest, to the exclusion of learning about new things. For example, I knew a youngster who became obsessed with vacuum cleaners and was reluctant to attend to or talk about anything else. Many autistic individuals also exhibit non-functional routines that appear superstitious in nature. One youngster I worked with had to hang every picture in the house at a crooked angle before he could use the toilet. Other youngsters might repetitively line up toy blocks, letters or numbers in a certain manner. Such autistic individuals may become very anxious or upset when changes or transitions are introduced. Youngsters may also demonstrate repetition in their use of language (repeating the same phrase over and over) or in their physical movements (e.g., repetitive hand flapping, body rocking, or twirling around and around.)

By definition, autism refers to difficulties in all three of the core symptom areas (social interaction, communication, repetitive behaviors). However, there are individuals who have difficulties in one or two areas, but not a third. As a result of the variety of symptom profiles across these three areas, researchers and clinicians often refer to them as "autistic spectrum disorders" rather than just referring to autism. Autistic spectrum disorders include autism (and high-functioning autism), Asperger's syndrome, and Pervasive Developmental Disorder-not otherwise specified (a category for individuals who meet some of the criteria for an autistic spectrum disorder, but do not fit neatly into a specific disorder like autism or Asperger's syndrome). Within the "autistic spectrum" there are individuals with no language and severe mental retardation, as well as people who are very articulate with gifted IQs, despite problems in social interaction and repetitive behaviors. For example, individuals with Asperger's syndrome have average to above average intellectual development, few or no problems with the structural use of language, but have problems in social interaction and repetitive behaviors.

Given the variety of symptoms and intellectual functioning among individuals with autistic spectrum disorders, a number of researchers have theorized about the core underlying problem within the disorders. Three, perhaps related, theories have received the most attention:

- Frith (1989) suggests that autistic individuals lack the ability to simultaneously integrate multiple language, social and emotional messages typically present in social situations. Something about their neurological functioning makes it difficult to assimilate and organize all the pertinent information. Since most social situations have multiple levels of sensory input, autistic individuals do not always fully grasp what is happening or how to respond. Instead, they may attend to and process only a fragment of the social experience, resulting in repetitive and atypical social behavior.
- Baron-Cohen (1995) suggests that the core problem is the inability to understand the thoughts and feelings of others, a process termed "theory of mind." Thus, autistic individuals have difficulty taking other people's perspectives.
- Hobson (1996) suggests that autism involves the inability to perceive and understand emotional expressions. This would then lead to difficulties in perspective taking and subsequent problems in social interaction.

These three theories can be considered complimentary. Both Baron-Cohen and Hobson's theories suggest that autistic individuals cannot easily empathize or understand another person's view of the world. Frith's theory helps explain why. The inability to simultaneously integrate information about what is happening in a social situation makes it difficult to imagine what others might be thinking and feeling. To take another's perspective, one has to synthesize information about the other person (e.g., the person's recent past experiences and preferences), along with what is happening to the person.

Most social skills rely on the ability to mentally adopt another person's perspective. For example, knowing why to say hello when you greet someone is based on understanding how others might think or feel if you ignore them rather than greet them. Knowing when to stop talking, take turns, respond to others' initiations, compromise, help others, or share, all come naturally when a person can easily take another's perspective. However, these social skills do not come naturally to autistic individuals, and must be taught explicitly. The Autism Social Skills Picture Book attempts to do just that, to breakdown social skills into their components and make explicit what to do and say in social situations.

The Importance of Visual Aides in Teaching Children with Autistic Spectrum Disorders

People with autism often have language and attention issues that interfere with their ability to learn from verbal explanations alone. As described earlier, many autistic individuals have difficulty comprehending language itself. For those others who have little trouble comprehending words, they may, nevertheless, have great difficulty staying attentive while learning tasks, especially if they become obsessively focused on their own area of interests. The benefits of using visual aides to facilitate greater understanding and comprehension among autistic students have been well documented (e.g., Quill, 1995). Most students, even those without disabilities, benefit from visual aides that back up a verbal explanation. This is because visual pictures (a) can make abstract verbal concepts more concrete, (b) remain stable over time, while auditory information can be missed as students' attention fluctuates, and (c) provide a more powerful means to engage attention.

The Autism Social Skills Picture Book uses a primarily visual strategy to teach social skills. Although the picture sets may benefit "typical" students, they will be particularly helpful for youngsters with auditory/language processing difficulties, difficulties in abstract thinking, and for those with difficulties sustaining attention. This includes children in the autistic spectrum, those with Attention Deficit/Hyperactivity Disorders, and individuals with learning disabilities.

TEACHING SOCIAL SKILLS

There are numerous strategies to teach social skills, all of which attempt to make explicit the social information and perspectives that may otherwise go unnoticed by autistic individuals. Described below are various strategies that have been used to teach social skills, as well as other behaviors. All of these approaches can incorporate the use of visual aides, such as picture books or modeling, to augment verbal instructions.

Discrete-Trial

This approach has been used to teach basic language, academic skills and rudimentary social skills. It is a highly directive method that often utilizes physical prompting and thus does not rely on the ability of the child to understand language. A discrete trial has at least four components: a cue, prompt, behavior, and reinforcement. As an example, consider teaching a youngster to make eye contact. A cue might be the phrase "look here" as I point to my eyes. The prompt might be to physically move his head so that he is looking at me. His behavior would be to either look at me or look away, and the reinforcement would come only when he looks at me.

Incidental Teaching

The term "incidental" refers to teaching a youngster about a social situation as it is occurring rather than in a structured lesson. The goal is to amplify the social environment for youngsters as it is unfolding so they pick up on the social cues and rules. This strategy works well in facilitating groups during unstructured communication and playtime.

Incidental teaching can be done very concretely for some children. Visual aides (e.g., using a turn card to denote whose turn it is during a game) or physical prompts (e.g., a tap on the shoulder to indicate their turn) are frequently used. Alternatively, incidental teaching can be more conceptual. For example, if a boy is talking non-stop about his obsession with light fixtures and his peers are starting to get restless, we might say to the boy, "Look how the other children are yawning and squirming in their seats. What do you think they are feeling? Why? Can you ask them if they want to hear more?" In contrast to this incidental lesson, we might later do a formal lesson on "Talking Briefly So Others Will Listen", using a visual picture-based format.

Cognitive Picture Rehearsal

This strategy utilizes cartoon-like drawings combined with positive reinforcement principles (Groden & Lavasseur, 1995). Cognitive picture rehearsal always includes drawings or pictures of three components: the antecedents to a problem situation, the targeted desired behavior, and a positive reinforcer. The pictures are displayed on index cards. On the back of each card is a script describing the sequence of events. Children are shown the sequence of cards until they can repeat what is happening in each picture. Then the sequence is reviewed just prior to the child entering the potentially problematic situation.

Unlike The Autism Social Skills Picture Book, which was designed to model general social skills, cognitive picture rehearsal is used for a specific problem situation. As an example, I had a seven-year-old group member who would run out of the office into the street whenever another member began to cry. We drew pictures of him watching another member crying (antecedent), then putting his fingers in his ears and going to a quiet area of the room (the desired behavior), then playing and getting his snack at the end of group (reinforcers). His mother would read the cards to him as a bedtime story and then again, just before our group session. Remarkably, we had no more incidents where he ran out of the group.

What are Social Stories?™

Developed by Carol Gray and colleagues (Gray et al.,1993), this strategy uses stories written in the first person to increase youngsters' awareness of problematic situations. Beginning with the child's understanding of a situation, a story is developed describing what is happening, why, and how people feel and think in the situation. The story contains directive statements (i.e., what to do in the situation), but the focus is on explaining what is happening in the situation.

Like cognitive picture rehearsal, Social Stories™ are read repeatedly to children until they have over-learned them, then read again just prior to the problematic situation. I have often used this strategy for youngsters with AS who believe they are being teased in a situation where they are not actually being teased. The story describes for the child what the accused teaser may be doing or thinking different from teasing. It may also contain ways to tell if the person really is teasing (e.g., the person is looking right at you and makes a critical remark). Social Stories are most effective when they very specifically explain how and why people behave and think in certain ways.

Structured Learning

This term refers to the strategies of Goldstein and colleagues in their "Skills Streaming" series (McGinnis & Goldstein, 1997). Structured learning contains four components: didactic instruction (explanation of the skill steps), modeling, role-playing with feedback, and practice in and outside the group.

The Skills Streaming series is an excellent resource that outlines steps for numerous skills. In addition, the format for teaching and promoting generalization is quite helpful. However, it does not contain many of the language pragmatic skills that are relevant for youngsters in the autistic spectrum, and it does not always explain specifically enough the steps or scripts that might be useful for individuals with autistic spectrum disorders.

The key to this approach, or any that relies partially on verbal instruction, is to engage the member's attention and make sure the language used is not too abstract. The Autism Social Skills Picture Book can be used quite successfully in combination with this structured learning method.

ABOUT SOCIAL SKILL PICTURE STORIES

What are Social Skill Picture Stories?

The Autism Social Skills Picture Book depicts, step by step, children demonstrating various social skills. Each skill is formatted sequentially, similar to a cartoon strip, with digital pictures of actual children combined with text and cartoon bubbles to denote what the children are saying – and sometimes thinking - as they engage in the skill. Included are the right (and sometimes the wrong) way to act with accompanying text that enhances the learning experience.

These pictures provide a means to compensate for the inherent difficulties many autistic individuals share. They make explicit what to do and say in social situations. In addition, by utilizing a picture format, they capitalize on students' visual processing strengths to facilitate attention and comprehension.

Reading The Autism Social Skills Picture Book is not a substitute for actually practicing skills. It is a useful tool in the initial acquisition of skills and should be followed with actual skill practice in the situations in which they are needed. If the goal is for a student to demonstrate a skill in a particular situation, then ultimately the student will need to repeatedly practice that skill in that situation. However, before students can physically practice a skill, they need some understanding of what to do. The Autism Social Skills Picture Book can facilitate that initial understanding. Furthermore, it promotes independence in that a student can refer to the book once a skill has been learned for further reinforcement of appropriate behaviors. The book can travel with a child across social environments, from home to school, through recess, or out into the community, thereby augmenting learning and further increasing independence.

The Autism Social Skills Picture Book helps youngsters visualize (a) the positive outcomes of performing a skill and (b) how people think and feel in response to their behaviors.

Who Should Use Social Skills Picture Stories?

Social skills picture stories will benefit most "typical" students by engaging attention and breaking down abstract skills into more concrete steps. They will be particularly helpful for youngsters who have difficulties with auditory/language processing, abstract thinking, or sustaining attention. This includes youngsters in the autistic spectrum as well as those with Attention Deficit/Hyperactivity Disorders and/or learning disabilities.

There is no age limit to using social skills picture stories. However, because of the age of the children depicted in this book, it is recommended that these pictures be used with children who have not yet reached adolescence. You can create your own social skills picture stories for any age group, including adults (See section on Making Your Own Social Skills Picture Stories).

How to Use This Book

Using social skills picture stories involves four stages: (1) initial instruction, (2) role-playing the skill, (3) reviewing the skill steps with corrective feedback, and (4) generalization. The first three stages can be repeated sequentially many times and are quite similar to the stages of "structured learning" described by Goldstein and colleagues in their Skills Streaming series (McGinnis & Goldstein, 1997). Structured learning contains four components: didactic instruction (explanation of the skill steps), modeling, role-playing with feedback, and practice for generalization. The difference here is that the didactic instruction and modeling stages are replaced by using the social skills picture stories. Using the picture stories results in less reliance on verbal instruction and instructor modeling.

Initial Instruction

Initial instruction involves the instructor (teacher, aide, or parent) reviewing a particular skill with the student until the student can explain or demonstrate it. Most skills contain a cover page, which is a text-only outline of the skill steps. Reading this page with a student is optional, and should be based on the developmental level of the student. For instance, this step can be left out for youngsters with very limited receptive language ability as it may lead to frustration and boredom. The instructor then shows each picture to the child and reads each skill step in order, describing what the individuals are doing, thinking and feeling.

The Autism Social Skills Picture Book is designed to reinforce learning through repetitive use of language and are attractive enough to maintain attention, despite repetitive use. The instructor can go through each page of a particular skill numerous times and then ask the student to relate what is happening in each picture. The instructor might ask questions such as "What is happening here? What is the first step? How is he feeling? What is he saying? What happens next?" For students who cannot describe what is happening, they can be asked to show each step (e.g., "Show me the picture where they make eye-contact. Now show me where they wait for a pause. Is this the right way or wrong way to say excuse me?").

Should You Teach the "Wrong Way" to Enact a Skill?

In many situations, the "Wrong Way" to enact a skill is presented. Depending on the personality and nature of the individual student, the instructor may choose not to explain or show the wrong way to enact a skill step and instead just focus on the right way to engage in the skill. If this is the case, the instructor can cover up the picture of the wrong way when going through the particular skill. The potential disadvantage of reviewing the wrong way is that some students are so entertained by inappropriate behavior that they may continually perform the skill the wrong way for their own or others' amusement. On the other hand, the advantage of demonstrating the wrong way is two-fold: (a) certain skills will be much better understood when both the right and wrong way are shown and (b) students who are reluctant to role-play may be more likely to try if they can role-play the wrong way first because then they do not have to fear making a mistake.

The bottom line is "know thy student." Youngsters who show a lot of "silly" attention seeking behaviors may not be good candidates for having the opportunity to role-play a skill the wrong way.

Role-playing the Skill

During the practice stage, the student is asked to act out the skill steps in the right order. The instructor reviews each skill step as shown in the book, prompting the student to role play each step. Role-playing is often more effective when done with two instructors or one instructor and two students. This way, the instructor can avoid participating in the role-play directly and act as a coach to help the students through the skill steps.

Role-play situations can begin with the exact situations depicted in this book, and then vary to address the situations most relevant to the students' daily lives.

Reviewing the Skill/Providing Corrective Feedback

After each role-play, the instructor should provide feedback about how each step was enacted. Feedback should always begin noting what was performed correctly and include ample praise. Avoid telling students directly that they performed a skill or step incorrectly. Instead, give corrective feedback by referring to the picture(s) and saying something like, "In this step, here is what I want you to do to perform the step even better." If needed, model the correct way to perform the skill. Corrective feedback and practice should continue until the student is able to demonstrate the step correctly.

The process of teaching a particular skill – reviewing the steps, role-playing the skill, and providing corrective feedback - should be repeated over and over until the student is able to demonstrate the skill without prompting. At this point, begin to promote generalization of the skill.

Generalization of Skills

Generalization comes with repeated practice of the skill in appropriate situations. Several ingredients are necessary to insure generalization: (1) opportunities to practice the skills across situations, (2) prompts, redirection, or baiting to use the skills, and (3) motivation to practice the skills.

Opportunities to practice the skills can be created in school, but often will occur naturally during the day. For example, "show & tell," lunch-time, or circle-time can be used daily to practice communication skills, while play skills can be practiced during "free-play time." At home, these skills can be prompted and practiced through planned play-dates or incidental (i.e., as the situation arises) communication with parents and siblings.

Once a teacher and student move into generalization of skills, it is important that consistency be maintained. All major caregivers for a particular student should be aware of the particular skill(s) being worked on, so that they can prompt that skill consistently across situations and offer similar corrective feedback.

Parents and teachers should be on the look-out for situations to prompt the student to use the skill. Instructors cannot wait for skill enactment to occur before rewarding the student, but rather parents and teachers must actively prompt and guide the youngster through the skill steps and then provide the token/reward. Initially, prompt only partial skill steps if a student has not fully mastered the entire sequence of the skill. This is referred to as *shaping*.

Another opportunity to prompt a skill is whenever the child "misbehaves." Every misbehavior is an opportunity to redirect the student to the appropriate way to get what she wants. Finally, "bait" certain skills. For example, an instructor may purposely fall down in front of a student to bait the skill "Showing Understanding for Other Peoples' Feelings." Or the instructor might take a student's pencil, then ask him to write something while the instructor talks to someone else. This is bait for "Interrupting," as the student will need to interrupt the conversation to ask for the pencil.

Motivating a student to use the new skill she is learning can be created through the use of a reward/token system. Students receive tokens for skill enactment that can be exchanged for rewards. Rewards might be snack items, privileges, toys, or free choice, and should always include praise. Often it is helpful to create a menu of rewards so that a student does not become satiated with a particular incentive. It is important that rewards be meaningful to the child. What is motivating to one student may have no effect on another. As skill acquisition takes place, efforts need to be made to fade out the external rewards. This can be done by substituting praise for tangible rewards, moving towards a more random ratio schedule of rewarding (which mirrors the natural consequences students get when there is no planned reward schedule), and pointing out to the student how positive skill enactment leads to positive natural consequences (e.g., the student did some of what he wanted, or a peer wanted to play the desired activity with the student).

MAKING YOUR OWN SOCIAL SKILLS PICTURE STORIES

Things to Consider

No set of skills can be complete for any individual, as the situations that demand social responses are constantly changing. Therefore, learning to make your own social skills picture stories and design skills to address specific situations allow you the greatest freedom.

Children can actively participate in the creation of new social skills picture stories by posing for pictures and assembling the books on paper or a computer. The benefits are doubled for youngsters who help to create their picture skills. They have the opportunity to role-play the skills during the picture taking, then have their attention drawn to a permanent, highly appealing record of themselves engaged in the skill.

In making your own picture stories, four areas need to be considered: (a) the target skill, (b) how to task analyze the skill, (c) what perceptions, thoughts, or feelings you want to highlight for the student, and (d) how to put the book together.

A. Identifying Target Skills

Parents, teachers, or students can identify target skills. Individualized skills can be patterned after one of the 20 skills depicted in this book, or a new skill can be developed that is based on a student's particular problematic behavior in a specific situation. Incorrect behaviors are often a clue to what behaviors need to be learned. When these behaviors occur, mentally ask, "Why or what was the student trying to achieve?" This process of determining the function of a behavior is called a functional assessment (see Durand, 1990).

The most common functions of a problem behavior are to:

- ESCAPE some task
- GET ATTENTION,
- provide SELF-STIMULATION,
- demand a TANGIBLE REWARD,
- DISPLACE ANGER from a previous situation,
- seek RETALIATION.

Whatever the function of the misbehavior, a crucial strategy to remedy the problem is to teach the student a more appropriate way to attain the desired reward or response. The appropriate alternative behavior can become the targeted skills for a new social skills picture sequence. Sample ideas for appropriate skills to teach for each proposed function of behavior are outlined below.

FUNCTION	INAPPROPRIATE BEHAVIOR	TARGET SKILLS
Escape	Tantrums, physical or verbal aggression, refusals.	Asking for a break, negotiating more time, asking for help to make the task easier. Trying when it's hard, dealing with mistakes.
Get Attention	Teasing, disruptive noises, inappropriate jokes or comments, complaints of being hurt.	Initiating communication or play, joining in communication or play, asking for help, asking to tell or show something to others.
Self-Stimulation	Rocking, hand flapping, twirling.	Performing the self-stimulatory behavior in a less disruptive way, alternative ways to relax or self-soothe.
Tangible Reward	Tantrums for a toy or privilege, refusing to cooperate with anything until reward is given.	Accept no for an answer or learn to wait for what you want, negotiating skills.
Displaced Anger	Verbal or physical aggression directed at the wrong person, refusal to cooperate with any instructions.	Identifying common sources of anger (e.g., someone yelled at or reprimanded the student) and learning to say how you feel to the person who upset you rather than act it out.
Retaliation	Teasing back, hitting back, stealing from someone who upset you.	Recognizing and appropriately expressing emotions, (i.e. Saying how you feel in a positive way "I feel ____, when you ____ because ____"). Telling someone to stop, ignoring, telling an authority.

B. Task Analysis

Task analyzing the skill simply means to break it up into smaller component steps. This will probably not be the same from student to student. Breaking down a skill too far will make it cumbersome to learn. Likewise, failure to break it down enough will lead to the student having difficulty learning the skill. As an example, imagine teaching "complimenting" as a skill and one of the steps was, "Say nice things about how the person looks." Some students would know what "nice things" are, but other students would need that step broken down further. We might create an interim step to show that "nice things to say" use the words "I like ____" and "Your ____ looks good." Pay attention to whether or not the student grasps a step being taught. If he is not learning or understanding the step, then it needs to be broken down further.

C. Perceptions, Thoughts and Feelings

Highlighting perceptions is a critical part of creating social skills picture stories. The better the student understands what people are thinking and feeling, the more likely he is to understand why to enact the skill. It is important to clearly demonstrate the benefit for the student to engage in the skill. Is it because it makes the other person happy and then the other person will give you something you want or play with you again? For example, the skill "Accepting No" illustrates that other people feel good when you accept no and that it is likely that you will get what you want later. Or "Dealing with Losing" teaches that others will be happy and play with you again if you do not get mad when you lose.

D. Assembling the Social Skills Picture Stories

Picture stories can be created several ways. Once a skill has been identified and the accompanying perceptions and verbalizations have been thought through, map out the skill steps and what pictures are needed. As often as possible, use the student as the model for the photographs. Pose students for the pictures while going through each skill step, first modeling what to do for each step. Do not worry if the student does not understand the skill fully at first, as learning will be reinforced after the picture set is created. The social skills picture stories included in this book were originally taken with a digital camera and then imported into a Microsoft Power Point presentation, where the bubbles and text were created. A similar process can be generated using a variety of suitable photograph software or desk-top publishing/ layout programs. Alternatively, pictures can be taken with a non-digital camera and pasted to paper. Bubbles and text can then be hand-written or typed onto colored paper and pasted onto the pictures. Be consistent in using one color for bubbles that express verbalizations and another color for thought/perception bubbles, so as not to confuse the student. Students can not only pose for the pictures, but can participate in the cutting, pasting and assembling of the skills. With some students, the exercise of sequencing the skill in the right order can be made into a game to further enhance the understanding of the individual steps.

Most importantly, creating new social skills picture stories - with or without the student - should be fun. Behavior modification can be a challenging task for many parents and teachers. Social skills picture stories are a creative and fun way to reduce the stress often associated with teaching alternative behaviors. Reduced stress can translate into better teaching and more progress for your child or student. So have fun and be creative.

Sample Steps for Other Skills

Two new skills are task analyzed for you below, followed by suggestions for other skills that might be appropriate for your child or a student with whom you work. Individualize the steps as needed to make them as user-friendly and meaningful as possible for the particular child.

Don't be the Rule Police!

- Do not tell other people what to do. It is not your job to make people follow the rules.
  If you tell other people what rules to follow or you tattle on them for not following rules, they may be annoyed with you.
- There are some exceptions when it is okay for you to tell people what rules to follow:
  When you are the teacher, boss, or put in charge of other people.
  When people ask you what the rules are.
  When people break a rule that could cause great danger to themselves or others.
  If people do something to hurt you, you can use the "I" statement or tell an adult what they have done.

Dealing with Specific Fears (also refer to Trying Something New for ideas)

- Tell someone that you are afraid, rather than run, scream or hide.
- Think to yourself, "I will feel better after I have tried it."
- Break down what you want to do into smaller, easier steps.
  If you are afraid to try a new food, try just looking at the food first, then watching others eat it, then smelling it, then licking it, then trying just a small bite of it.
- Find something calming you can do while trying to overcome your fear.
  Try holding a stuffed animal, taking deep breaths or reading a book.
- Go through each step in bullet number three while engaging in the calming activity.
- Receive a reward and praise for taking any steps towards facing the fear.

Dealing with Specific Triggers to Anger

- Refer to Accepting No for an Answer, Dealing with Mistakes, or Dealing with Teasing for ideas

Becoming More Flexible when Change Occurs

- Refer to Compromising for ideas

Stopping a Favored Activity

- Refer to Accepting No for an Answer for ideas

REFERENCES

Baron-Cohen, S. (1995). <u>Mindblindness</u>. Cambridge, MA: The MIT Press.

Durand, V.M. (1990). <u>Severe behavior problems: A functional communication training approach</u>. New York: Guilford Press.

Frith, U. (1989). <u>Autism: Explaining the enigma</u>. Oxford, England: Blackwell.

Gray, C.(1993). <u>The new social story book - illustrated edition</u>. Arlington, TX: Future Horizons, Inc.

Grodon, J. & LeVasseur, P. (1995). <u>Cognitive picture rehearsal: A system to teach self-control</u>. In K. A. Quill (Ed.) (1995), <u>Teaching Children with Autism</u>. Albany, NY: Delmar Publishing.

Hobson, R.P. (1996). <u>Autism and the development of the mind</u>. Mahwah, NJ: Lawrence Erlbaum Associates.

McGinnis, E. & Goldstein, A. (1997). <u>Skillstreaming the elementary school child: New strategies and perspectives for teaching prosocial skills</u>. Champaign, IL: Research Press.

Quill, K. A. (Ed.) (1995), <u>Teaching children with autism</u>. Albany, NY: Delmar Publishing.

PART TWO

COMMUNICATION

RELATED

SKILLS

Don't Be a Space Invader

One of the hidden social rules of conversation is to stand or sit an appropriate distance away from the person. Sitting or standing too close is referred to as 'invading their space.'

- **Stand at least an arm's length away when talking with another person.**

- **Don't get too close.**
  (An exception is when talking with your mom or dad or a close relative.)

Don't be a space invader when you want to play with other kids or adults.

Right Way

They are at least an arm's length away while they talk.

Wrong Way

The boy is too close. He is being a space invader.

Don't be a space invader when you say, "Hi" to other people.

Right Way

They are at least an arm's length away.

Wrong Way

The boy is too close to his teacher.
He is being a space invader.

■ Don't be a space invader when you stand in a line.

Right Way

They leave some space between each other.

Wrong Way

The kids are too close to each other.
They are being space invaders.

HINT Sometimes you have no choice but to be too close to other people, like when you are in a crowded elevator or on a crowded bus or train. That's OK. But when you do have the room, make sure you keep some space between you and the other person.

Don't be a space invader when you are talking with your teacher.

Right Way

The boy is at least an arm's length away from the teacher.

Wrong Way

The students are too close to the teacher. They are being space invaders.

Listening Position

When someone else is talking, it's important to be a good listener. That involves your mind and your body. This skill is about what your body should do when listening.

- **Make eye contact.**

- **Quiet hands and feet. Stay still.**

- **Quiet mouth. Don't talk while other people are talking.**

■ Make eye contact with the person talking.

Right Way

They are looking at him.

Wrong Way

They are not looking at him.

HINT It helps to turn your body toward the person talking.

■ Quiet hands and feet. Stay still; don't move around or walk around.

Right Way	**Wrong Way**
They are staying still.	They are moving their feet and hands.

Quiet mouth. Don't talk while other people are talking.

Right Way

They are not talking while the girl in the chair talks.

Wrong Way

They are all talking at the same time the girl is talking.

Interrupting I - Help with opening a jar

- **Sometimes it is okay to interrupt people who are busy or are talking.**
  If you need help, information or guidance
  If there is an emergency
  If you want something

- **Walk up to the person(s) and wait for a pause in their conversation or activity.**

- **Say, "Excuse me..." then ask for what you want or need.**

- **Wait for their response.**

- **Say, "Thank You" before leaving.**

Decide if you need to interrupt someone, because you need help, information or you want something.

The boy can't open the jar. He will interrupt the teachers and ask for help.

Walk up to the person(s) and wait for a pause. A pause is when others stop talking.

Right Way

The boy walked up to the teachers and is waiting for them to stop talking and look at him.

Wrong Way

The boy did not wait for them to stop talking. He grabbed the teacher's arm.

Say, "Excuse me..." then ask for what you need or want.

Right Way

The boy says, "Excuse me" and asks for help.

Wrong Way

The boy did not say, "Excuse me" or ask for help. He just grabbed the teacher.

Wait for their response. Then say, "Thank you" before leaving.

The boy waited for the teachers to help him open the jar.

Interrupting II - Help with a zipper

- **Sometimes it is okay to interrupt people who are busy or are talking.**
  If you need help, information or guidance
  If there is an emergency
  If you want something

- **Walk up to the person(s) and wait for a pause in their conversation or activity.**

- **Say, "Excuse me..." then ask for what you want or need.**

- **Wait for their response.**

- **Say, "Thank you" before leaving.**

Decide if you need to interrupt someone, because you need help, information or you want something.

The girl can't zip up her coat. She will interrupt the teachers and ask for help.

■ Walk up to the person(s) and wait for a pause. A pause is when others stop talking.

Right Way

The girl walked up to the teachers and is waiting for them to stop talking and look at her.

Wrong Way

The girl did not wait for them to stop talking. She grabbed the teacher's arm to get her attention.

Say, "Excuse me..." then ask for what you need or want.

Right Way

The girl says "Excuse me" and asks for help.

Wrong Way

The girl did not say, "Excuse me" or ask for help. She just grabbed the teacher.

Wait for their response. Then say, "Thank you" before leaving.

The girl waited for the teacher to help her zip her coat.

Interrupting III - Asking Peers for a Toy

- **Sometimes it is okay to interrupt people who are busy or are talking.**
  If you need help, information or guidance
  If there is an emergency
  If you want something

- **Walk up to the person(s) and wait for a pause in their conversation or activity.**

- **Say, "Excuse me..." then ask for what you want or need.**

- **Wait for their response.**

- **Say, "Thank you" before leaving.**

Decide if you need to interrupt someone, because you need help, information or you want something.

The boy wants to play with one of the dinosaurs.
He will need to interrupt the girls.

Walk up to the person(s) and wait for a pause. A pause is when others stop talking.

Right Way

The boy walked up to the girls and is waiting for them to stop talking and look at him.

Wrong Way

The boy did not wait for them to stop playing. He grabbed the girl's shoulder to get her attention.

Say, "Excuse me..." then ask for what you need or want.

Right Way

The boy says, "Excuse me" and asks to play with the dinosaur.

Wrong Way

The boy did not say, "Excuse me" or ask to play with the dinosaur. He just tried to take the dinosaur.

Wait for their response. Then say, "Thank you" before leaving.

The boy waited for the girls to give him the dinosaur.

Greetings

- It is friendly and polite to say, "Hello" or some other form of greeting when you see someone you know during the day.

- In the morning, the first time you see someone you should say, "Good morning."

- When you pass someone in the hallway, say, "Hi."

- When someone is leaving for the day, you can say, "Bye", "Goodbye" or "See you later."

The first time you see someone each day, you should say, "Hello" or "Hi."

The first time the students see their teacher during the day, they say, "Hi" or "Hello."

HINT   Sometimes it is polite and friendly to say "hello" to people you don't know very well, like a new teacher, the principal, the clerk at the grocery store, or the person at your favorite fast food restaurant. You should say, "hello" the first time you see them during the day, **not** every time you see them in the same day.

In the morning, the first time you see someone you should say, "Good morning."

Right Way

The first time the student sees her teacher in the morning, she says, "Good morning."

Wrong Way

The first time the girl sees her teacher in the morning, she says nothing.

HINT Smile and make eye contact when you greet the person.

When you pass someone in the hall, say, "Hi."

Right Way

They pass by each other and say, "Hi."

Wrong Way

They pass by each other and do not say, "Hi."

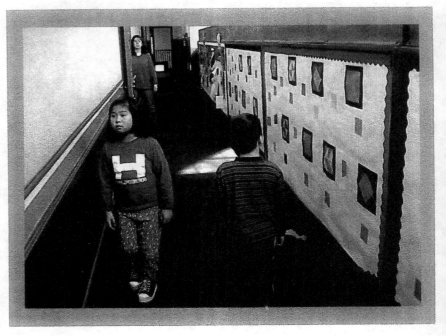

HINT Smile and make eye contact when you greet the person. It's okay to add a brief wave of your hand too.

When someone is leaving for the day, you should say, "Goodbye", "Bye" or "See you later."

Right Way	Wrong Way
The girl is leaving, so she says, "Goodbye."	The girl is leaving, but she forgets to say anything to her teacher.

When someone is leaving for the day, you should say, "Goodbye", "Bye" or "See you later."

Right Way

Dr. Baker is leaving, so the students say, "Bye" and "See you later."

Wrong Way

Dr. Baker is leaving, but the students ignore him. No one says goodbye.

HINT   Make eye contact with the person leaving and smile.

Listening (during a conversation)

- **Make eye contact with the person talking.**

- **Stay still and quiet.**

- **Wait for a pause in the conversation before saying something. A pause is when others stop talking.**

- **Ask a question about what the other person is saying to show your interest.**

■ Make eye contact.

Right Way

The students are looking at the boy talking.

Wrong Way

They are looking around the room. They are not looking at the boy talking.

Stay still and quiet while the person is talking.

Right Way

The students are staying still in their seats and are quietly listening to the boy talk.

Wrong Way

They are moving around and making noise.

HINT   It is okay to nod your head or smile at times to show the person talking that you are listening.

Wait for a pause. That means, do not talk when the other person is talking.

Right Way	Wrong Way
The students are not talking while the boy with the dinosaur talks.	The are all talking at the same time as the boy is talking.

Example 1: Ask a question about what the other person is saying to show your interest.

Right Way	**Wrong Way**
The girl waited for a pause, and then asked a WHAT question about the dinosaur.	None of the students are showing good listening skills. The girl is not asking a question about the dinosaur.

Example 2: Ask a question about what the other person is saying to show your interest.

Right Way

The girl waited for a pause, and then asked a WHERE question about the dinosaur.

Wrong Way

None of the students are showing good listening skills. The girl is not asking a question about the dinosaur.

Example 3: Ask a question about what the other person is saying to show your interest.

Right Way

The boy waited for a pause, and then asked a HOW question about the dinosaur.

Wrong Way

None of the students are showing good listening skills. The boy is not asking a question about the dinosaur.

Starting and Maintaining a Conversation I (about the present)

You can start a conversation in many ways. One way is to talk about something that is happening in the present moment.

- **When you see someone for the first time during the day, greet him or her. (See Greetings, page 31)**

- **Ask a question about what he or she is doing.**
  What are you eating?
  What are you playing?
  What are you reading?
  What are you getting?

- **Ask follow-up questions about the activity, using WHO, WHAT, WHERE, WHY and HOW.**

When you see someone for the first time during the day, say, "Hi" or "Hello" and ask, "How are you?"

HINT

See Greetings, page 31.
Remember to make eye contact and smile.

Example 1: **Ask a question about what they are doing.**

When *someone is eating*

Ask follow-up questions about the activity.
(WHO, WHAT, WHERE, WHEN, WHY and HOW questions.)

Example 2: Ask a question about what they are doing.

When someone is playing

Ask follow-up questions about the activity.
(WHO, WHAT, WHERE, WHEN, WHY and HOW questions.)

Example 3: Ask a question about what they are doing.

When someone *is* reading

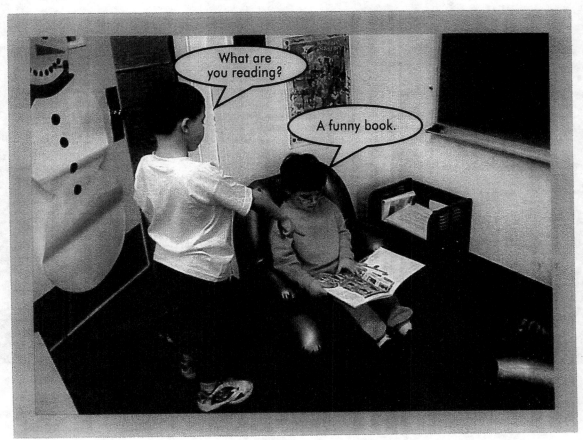

Ask follow-up questions about the activity.
(WHO, WHAT, WHERE, WHEN, WHY and HOW questions.)

Example 4: Ask a question about what they are doing.

When someone *is* getting something.

Ask follow-up questions about the activity.
(WHO, WHAT, WHERE, WHEN, WHY and HOW questions.)

Starting and Maintaining a Conversation II (about the past)

You can start a conversation in many ways. One way is to talk about something that is happening in the past, either earlier in the day or in previous days.

- **When you see someone for the first time during the day, greet him or her. (See Greetings, page 31)**

- **Ask a question about what he did.**
  "What did you do today? What did you play today?"

Some other questions might be:
  "Who did you see today? What did you do over the weekend?
  How was school today?"

- **Ask follow-up questions, using WHO, WHAT, WHERE, WHY and HOW.**

When you see someone for the first time during the day, say, "Hi" or "Hello" and ask, "How are you?"

HINT

See Greetings, page 31.
Remember to make eye contact and smile. Don't stand too close to the other person; give him his space.

Ask a question about what he did.

Ask follow up questions. (WHO, WHAT, WHERE, WHEN, WHY and HOW questions.)

Ask follow up questions. (WHO, WHAT, WHERE, WHEN, WHY and HOW questions.)

To keep the conversation going, ask another question. (WHO, WHAT, WHERE, WHEN, WHY and HOW questions.)

Ask follow up questions. (WHO, WHAT, WHERE, WHEN, WHY and HOW questions.)

Ask follow up questions. (WHO, WHAT, WHERE, WHEN, WHY and HOW questions.)

Ask follow up questions. (WHO, WHAT, WHERE, WHEN, WHY and HOW questions.)

Ask follow up questions. (WHO, WHAT, WHERE, WHEN, WHY and HOW questions.)

Ask follow up questions. (WHO, WHAT, WHERE, WHEN, WHY and HOW questions.)

Ending a Conversation

Sometimes you may want to end a conversation with another person. A few reasons you might want to do this are:
    You are bored.
    It's time for you to leave.
    You want to talk about something else or do something else.

- **Decide if you want to end the conversation.**

- **Wait until you have asked at least one question and the person has answered it.**

- **Say, "It was nice talking with you, but I have other things I have to do right now. See you later."**

The boy with the hat is telling the other boys a story about fishing.

▪ Decide if you want to end the conversation.

One boy is feeling bored. It is almost time for the other boy to leave. They both want to end the conversation.

HINT When you are talking with someone else, make sure to stop periodically and see if they are still interested in what you are talking about. See Talking Briefly, page 79.

69

Wait until you have asked at least one question and the person has answered it.

Right Way

The boy is asking a question to show he is interested.

Wrong Way

The boys just walk away without asking any questions to show they were interested.

The two boys each ask one more question before they end the conversation.

HINT   It makes the other person feel like you care when you ask questions.

Say, "It was nice talking with you, but I have other things I have to do right now. See you later."

Right Way

The boy explains why he must stop talking and says goodbye.

Wrong Way

The boys just walk away without saying goodbye or explaining why they are leaving.

Or, you could say, "It was nice talking with you, but I have to go home now. See you later."

Right Way

The boy explains why he must stop talking and says goodbye.

Wrong Way

The boys just walk away without saying goodbye or explaining why they are leaving.

Introducing Yourself

- There are some times when you need to meet other people you don't know. This is a time to introduce yourself to the other person(s).

- Wait for a pause in the conversation, if she is talking.

- Walk up to the person, stand about an arm's length away, and make good eye contact.

- Say, "My name is _____. What's your name?" Wait for his answer.

- Say, "It's nice to meet you" and shake hands.

Look for an opportunity to introduce yourself to someone you don't know.

The teacher is bringing a new student to the class.
The other children should meet him.

Wait for a pause in the conversation, if she is talking.

The boy is waiting for the teacher to stop talking.

▪ **Walk up to the person, stand about an arm's length away, and make good eye contact.**

Right Way

The boy walked up to the other boy, stood about an arm's length away, and looked at him.

Wrong Way

The boy did not look at the other boy.

HINT   Smiling at the other person will make him feel more welcomed.

Say, "My name is _____. What's your name? " Wait for his response.

HINT   Remember to keep eye contact while you're introducing yourself.

Say, "It's nice to meet you" and shake hands.

Right Way

The boy is about an arm's length away, shakes his hand, and says "It's nice to meet you."

Wrong Way

The boy gets too close to the person he just met and hugs him instead of offering to shake his hand.

Ouch!

HINT Shake hands with your right hand. Don't shake too hard or too long. About 3 shakes is appropriate. Hugging someone you don't know, even a person your own age, is not appropriate behavior.

Knowing When to Stop Talking (Talking Briefly)

- Look for signs that indicate that the other person is interested in your topic.

- If the other person looks bored or not interested, ask, "Do you want to hear more?"

- If the other person does not want to hear more, then stop talking or ask, "What do you want to talk about now?"

Adam, the boy on the left with the book, is talking about fish. Paul, the other boy, looks interested.

Adam   Paul

HINT Clues that show that Paul is interested: He is looking at the book. His body is turned toward Adam.

Look for signs that indicate the other person is interested in your topic.

Right Way

Adam pauses frequently to see if Paul is still interested in what he is saying.

Adam   Paul

Wrong Way

Adam keeps talking and does not look at Paul to check if he is still interested in fish.

Adam   Paul

HINT   Clues that show Paul is bored: His body is turned away from Adam. He is looking around the room. His facial expression shows that he is bored.

If the other person looks bored or not interested, ask, "Do you want to hear more?"

Right Way

Adam sees that Paul is bored, so he asks if he wants to hear more about fish.

Adam   Paul

Wrong Way

Adam keeps talking and does not ask if Paul is still interested in the topic of fish.

Adam   Paul

■ **If the other person does not want to hear more, then stop talking, or ask, "What do you want to talk about now?"**

Right Way	**Wrong Way**
Adam asks Paul what he wants to talk about.	Adam keeps talking and does not ask Paul if he is still interested.

Adam   Paul

Adam   Paul

HINT If you do not want to change topics, or don't want to talk about the new topic he suggests, then try compromising (See Compromising, page 103)

PLAY

RELATED

SKILLS

Asking Someone to Play

- Find something to play.

- Walk up to someone with whom you want to play.

- Wait for the other person to look at you.

- Ask, "Do you want to play?"

Find something to play.

The boy wants to play the game Operation.

Walk up to someone with whom you want to play.

The boy walked up to the other boy.
He brought the game with him.

■ Wait for the other person to look at you.

The boy waited for the other boy to look at him.

HINT   Remember to make eye contact
with the other person.

Ask, "Do you want to play?"

HINT Smile when you ask someone to play with you. It makes you look friendly. Show the other person what you want him to play with you.

Joining in Play

- Decide if you want to join others who are playing.

- Walk up to the person and wait for a pause in their play.

- Ask if you can play. Say, "Can I play too?"

- If they say, "No" ask someone else to play.

Decide if you want to join others who are playing.

The boy is watching them play and would like
to join them.

Walk up to the person and wait for a pause in their play.

The boy is waiting for them to take a break so he
can ask to join in.

Ask if you can play. Say, "Can I play too?"

Right Way

The boy walked up to them and asked if he could play.

Wrong Way

The boy grabbed the ball without asking.

If they say, "No", ask someone else to play.

They are not letting him play, so he should ask someone else to play.

If they say, "No", ask someone else to play.

Right Way

The boy walked up to someone else and asked if he could play.

Wrong Way

When they said, "No", the boy grabbed the ball and ran with it.

Sharing

- **Think about the reasons to share.**
  It will make them happy.
  Sharing shows them that I like them.
  Friends share with other friends.

- **Offer to share something you have.**

- **If someone asks you to share something that you have, share it with her.**

Think about the reasons to share.

If the teacher shares the pretzels, the other teacher and the girl will be happy. They will share food with her sometime.

Offer to share something you have.

Right Way

The teacher offered the girl a pretzel.

Wrong Way

The teacher did not share any pretzels.

If someone asks you to share something that you have, share it with her.

Right Way

The girl let the other girl see her toy.

Wrong Way

The girl did not share her toy.

Compromising

- **Ask the other person what he wants to do.**

  Say, "What do you want to play?"
  Wait and listen for his response.

- **Tell the other person what you want to do.**

- **If you want to do different things, then compromise.**

  Offer to do some of what he wants to do and then some of what you want to do.

- **Do some of what he wants to do. Then do some of what you want to do.**

Ask the other person what he wants to do. Wait and listen for his response.

Tell the other person what you want to do.

If you want to do different things, then compromise. Offer to do some of what he wants to do and then some of what you want to do.

Right Way

They decide to compromise and play some Candyland and then some Operation.

Wrong Way

They do not compromise and cannot agree on what to play.

Do some of what he wants to do and then do some of what you want to do.

Right Way

They compromise and play some Candyland and then some Operation.

Wrong Way

They did not compromise and now the boy has no one to play with.

Taking Turns During Play

When you are playing with another person, or a group of people, everyone wants to have a chance to play. You must make sure that you take your own turn, and give other people a turn, also.

- **Let other people play while you wait.**

- **Think to yourself, "If I wait, then I will get a turn."**

- **When you wait, others will feel happy and want to give you a turn.**

Let others play while you wait.

Paul   Sam   Adam

The two boys are waiting while Paul has a turn at bat.

Think to yourself, "If I wait, then I will get a turn, too."

Right Way

The boys think that if they wait, they will get a turn at bat.

Paul   Sam   Adam

Wrong Way

The boys don't wait their turn. They try to take the bat away.

Paul   Sam   Adam

When you wait, others will feel happy and want to give you a turn.

Right Way

Sam waited, and now it is his turn.

Paul   Sam   Adam

Wrong Way

The boys did not wait,
so they will not get a turn.

Paul   Sam   Adam

Now Sam gets a turn to bat while the other boys wait.

Sam   Adam   Paul

The two boys are waiting while Sam has a turn at bat.

Think to yourself, "If I wait, then I will get a turn, too."

Right Way	Wrong Way
The boys think that if they wait, they will get a turn at bat.	Adam doesn't wait his turn. He tries to take the bat away.

Sam   Adam   Paul

Sam   Adam   Paul

When you wait, others will feel happy and want to give you a turn.

Right Way

Adam waited, and now it is his turn.

Sam   Adam

Wrong Way

Adam did not wait.
Now he will not get a turn.

Sam   Adam   Paul

Now Adam gets a turn to play while the other boys wait.

Adam   Paul and Sam

The two boys are waiting while Adam has a turn at bat.

■ The boys are happy because everyone waited for their turn.

They shake hands at the end of the game
because they are friends.

HINT   Instead of shaking hands, everyone might give a
"high five" to each other, or say, "That was fun!"

Playing a Game

- **Ask how to play the game.**

  Say, "How do you play this game?"

- **Decide who will go first.**
  - Let the other person go first. Say, "You can go first."
  - If there are more than two people, you can play "Odd Finger is It" to decide who goes first.
  - You can also roll dice. The person with the highest roll of the dice gets to go first. With two people, you can roll dice or flip a coin.
  - Or you can play "Odds or Evens."

- **Take turns.**

The teacher is asking the boy and girl if they want to play tag.

Ask how to play the game.

The kids ask how to play the game and the teacher explains it to them.

Decide who will go first.

All the kids want to go first. They will find a fair
way to **decide** who will go first.

Decide who will go first.

The kids decide to play "Odd finger is It" to decide who will go first. On the count of three, each child puts one or two fingers out. If one person has a different number of fingers out than everyone else, that person gets to go first. If everyone has the same number of fingers out, try it again until one is different.

■ Take turns.

They are taking turns being "It."

124

Dealing with Losing

Sometimes when you play a game with a friend, you win the game. Sometimes, though, you lose the game, and losing doesn't feel too good. It might make you upset. You might get mad or even sad. When that happens, it's important to know how to deal with losing. This lesson will help you.

- **Think to yourself, "It's only a game. There will be other games."**

- **Think, "Even if I lose the game, I can keep or win a friend if I do not get mad."**

- **Say, "Good game."**

John and Phil are playing Tic Tac Toe on the board.

John   Phil

John loses the game to Phil.

John   Phil

▓ Think to yourself, "It's only a game. There will be other games."

Right Way	**Wrong Way**
John realizes that it's only a game, and he will get to try again.	John does not realize that he can try again, so he stays angry and sad.

HINT

To help John calm down so he doesn't stay mad, see Keeping Calm, page 135.

Think, "Even if I lose the game, I can keep or win a friend if I do not get mad.

Right Way	**Wrong Way**
John realizes that he will win a friend if he does not get mad.	John stays mad and angry.

■ Say, "Good game!"

Right Way

John did not get mad and says,
"Good game, Phil."

John   Phil

Wrong Way

John is still angry and may
lose a friend.

John   Phil

HINT

To help John calm down so he doesn't stay mad,
see Keeping Calm, page 135.

Phil and John will stay friends and play together again, if John stays calm and does not get mad.

Right Way

Phil wants to play with John again because John did not get mad.

John   Phil

Wrong Way

Phil does not want to play with John again because John got mad when he lost.

John   Phil

EMOTION
RELATED
SKILLS

Keeping Calm

Sometimes events occur that make you feel angry, sad, anxious, or many other ways that are not comfortable. This lesson will help you learn to stay calm when these situations happen.

- **Stop and count to ten.**
  1...2...3...4...5...6...7...8...9...10

- **Take 3 deep breaths.**

- **Do something fun to feel better.**
  Draw, play a game, watch TV, or listen to music.

- **Tell someone how you feel.**
  I feel sad because...
  I'm angry because...

The boy did something wrong and he is told to go sit at his desk.

The boy feels sad that he did something the teacher didn't like. He feels angry, too, because he was told to sit down.

The boy wants to help himself calm down. He will stop and count to 10.

Right Way

The boy stops and counts to 10.

Wrong Way

The boy does not stop to calm himself, and stays angry.

■ Take 3 deep breaths.

Right Way	**Wrong Way**
The boy takes 3 deep breaths.	The boy stays sad and angry.

■ Do something fun to feel better.

Right Way

The boy draws to feel better.

Wrong Way

The boy stays sad and angry.

Tell someone how you feel.

Right Way

The boy tells his friend how he feels.

Wrong Way

The boy does nothing to calm himself.
He stays sad and angry.

Showing Understanding for Other People's Feelings

Other people have their own feelings that may or may not be the same as ours. When we notice other people's feelings and offer to help, we are said to be "understanding." Being understanding is a good quality and helps us make and keep friends.

- **Look for signs that other people are sad, angry or need help.**
  Look at their face? Are they frowning or crying? Look at their body posture. Are they slumping down in their chair? Do they have their head down on the desk? Are they covering their ears with their hands?

- **Ask, "Are you okay?" Then ask, "What happened?"**

- **Ask if you can help. Say, "Can I help?"**

- **If they say, "Yes", then do something to help.**

Example 1: A boy is getting upset because he is having a hard time doing his school work.

Look for signs that others are sad, angry or need help.

HINT

Clues that something might be wrong with the boy:
He's slumped down in his chair. His eyes are looking down.
The corners of his mouth are turned down; he's frowning.
He's not talking with anyone or doing anything.

Ask, "Are you okay? What happened?"

Ask if you can help.

If they say, "Yes", do something to help.

The girl is helping the boy with his school work.

The boy feels happy and likes the girl for helping him.

Example 2: A boy fell down and looks hurt.

Look for signs that others are sad, angry or need help.

HINT   Signs that show the boy may need some help:
He is lying on the floor. He is holding his shoulder.
His facial expression looks like he's in pain.

Ask, "Are you okay? What happened?"

Ask if you can help.

If they say, "Yes", do something to help.

The boy helped him get up off the floor.

Example 3: **The boy is sad. He got some M&M's® candies, but then he dropped them on the floor.**

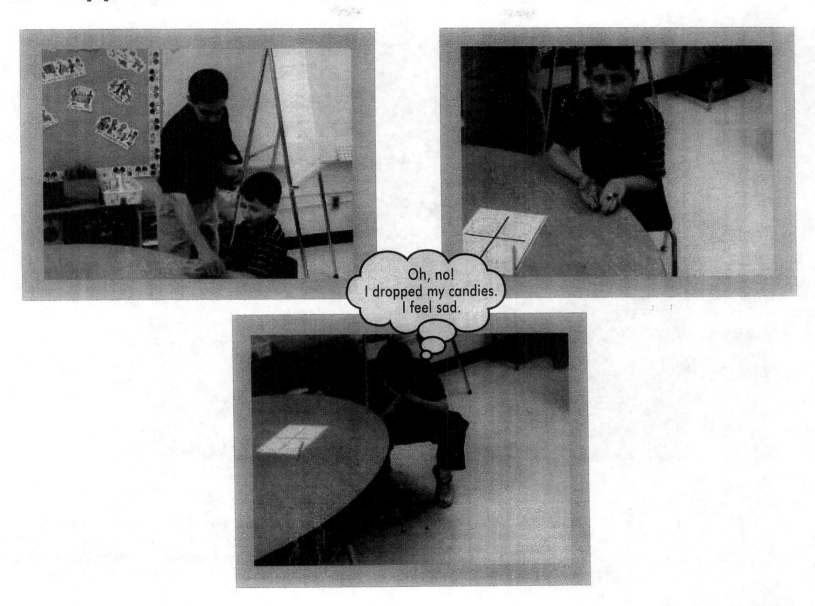

Look for signs that others are sad, angry or need help.

HINT

Signs that show the boy may be sad:
He is looking down at the floor. His head is propped up in his hand. He's pointing to something on the floor. His mouth is turned down. He doesn't look happy.

Ask, "Are you okay? What happened?"

Ask if you can help.

If they say, "Yes", then do something to help.

The boy got him more M&M's® candies.

Accepting "No" for an Answer

- **Sometimes teachers and parents say, "No" when you ask for something.**
    "Mom, can I have a cookie?"
    "No, it's too close to dinner time."

- **Accept "No" by saying "Okay" and do not get mad.**
    Sometimes this is not easy to do, especially when you really want something.

- **If you do not get mad* and accept "No" for an answer, the other person will feel good about you.**
    She may give you some of what you want later, or let you do something you want to do later.

* If you do get mad, then look at page 135, Keeping Calm.

Sometimes people say, "No" when you ask them for something.

When the boy asks to play the game, the teacher says,
"No", and tells him to do his work first.

Accept "No" by saying, "Okay" and do not get mad.

Right Way

The boy says, "Okay", and does not get mad. He knows he will get to play the game later.

Wrong Way

The boy gets mad and does not accept "No" for an answer.

If you accept "No", then the other person will be happy. She may let you do something you want to do later.

Right Way

The boy now gets to play because he waited until he finished his work.

Wrong Way

The boy still can't play because he would not accept "No" and wait to play.

Dealing with Mistakes

Everyone makes mistakes. We make mistakes at school, at home, when we're out at a restaurant, or out in the community. Some mistakes are little mistakes, like adding a number wrong, while other mistakes are bigger mistakes, like breaking your brother's toy or one of mom's lamps, or telling a lie. It's impossible to be perfect and not make mistakes. What's important is to learn from our mistakes.

- **Tell yourself, "It's okay to make a mistake. That's how we learn."**

- **Try the task again.**

- **Ask for help if you need it.**

- **Tell yourself you did a good job learning from your mistake.**

The teacher tells the boy to do some math work.

The boy is trying to do the work.

The boy makes a mistake in doing his work.

Tell yourself, "It's okay to make a mistake. That's how we learn."

Right Way

The boy knows that he can learn from his mistake.

Wrong Way

The boy gets nervous because he thinks it's not okay to make mistakes.

■ Try the task again.

Right Way

The boy tries to do the work again.
He wants to get it right.

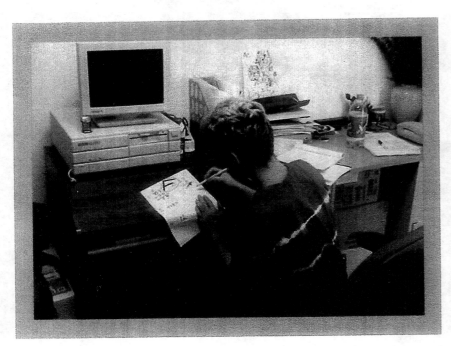

Wrong Way

The boy gets so mad, he wants to quit.

HINT   Sometimes we have to try again and again before we get something right. It's important to keep trying and not give up!

Ask for help if you need it.

Right Way

The boy asks for help with his math, instead of getting mad because he's making mistakes.

Wrong Way

The boy gets mad instead of asking for help.

The teacher helps the boy.

Tell yourself you did a good job learning from your mistakes.

Trying Something New

It's good to try new things. That might be a new kind of food, a new game, a new sport, or a different way to walk to the park. Sometimes we like the new things we try, but sometimes we don't. That's okay. What's important is to try it.

- **If you are afraid to try something new, talk about it with someone.**

  Tell yourself, "It's okay to be afraid the first few times. After I try it, I will feel better."

- **Calm yourself with a favorite activity.**

- **Watch others try it.**

- **Ask someone to explain how to do it.**

- **Try it yourself.**

The boy wants to play with his friends, but he is feeling afraid to try the new game.

HINT If you're feeling afraid to make a mistake, see Dealing with Mistakes, page 165.

If you are afraid to try something new, talk about it with someone.

The boy decides to talk with his teacher about his feelings.

■ **Tell yourself, "It's okay to be afraid. After I try it, I will feel better."**

HINT The boy is showing courage by being willing to try the game, even when he is afraid.

Calm yourself with a favorite activity.

The boy reads a book to calm down.

Watch other people try the game. Ask questions if you do not understand.

The boy watches the other boys play the game until he feels okay. He asks them about the game.

The boy tries playing the game with the other boys.

The boy feels happy he tried something new.

Dealing with Teasing

- Ask if the person is teasing you.

- If he is, tell the person to STOP in a strong voice.

- If he keeps teasing, tell him you do not care what he says.

- If he keeps teasing, ignore him or walk away.

- If he keeps teasing, tell an adult.

The boy is teasing the other boy about his sneakers.

HINT

Some teasing is friendly and some teasing is meant to hurt our feelings. If you don't understand the difference, make sure to ask your mom or dad or a teacher to explain it to you.

Ask if he is teasing you.

☐ Tell him to STOP in a strong voice.

HINT   Make eye contact with the person and hold
out your hand at arms length, to indicate
STOP to the other person.

If he keeps teasing, tell him you do not care what he says.

If he keeps teasing, ignore him or walk away.

HINT   In this situation, it is okay to turn your
back to the other person.

If he keeps teasing, tell an adult.

Trying When Work is Hard

Some things are easy to do, but other things may be hard to do. This might be one of your subjects at school, learning a new game, or trying a new sport or outdoor activity. It's important to keep trying, even when something is hard to do. This is called having perseverance.

- **Try to do the work.**

- **Ask for help if you need it.**

- **Ask for a short break if you start getting upset.**

- **Go back to doing your work. Try again.**

■ Try to do the work.

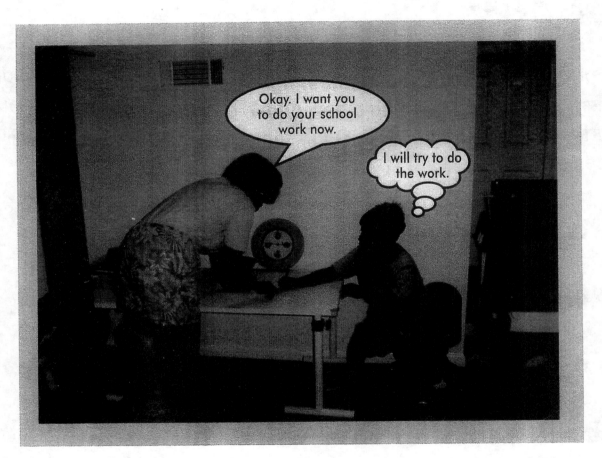

The teacher tells the boy to start his work. He tries to do it.

Ask for help if you need it.

Right Way

The boy asks for help when he has trouble with the work.

Wrong Way

The boy is having trouble doing the work. He gets mad.

If you start getting upset, ask for a short break to get calm again.

Right Way

The boy asks for a break when he starts to feel upset.

Wrong Way

The boy gets upset and tears up his work.

The boy has a five minute break.

HINT   Use your break to calm down. Do something that makes you calm, like read, play with a favorite toy, listen to music, or take deep breaths. (See Keeping Clam, page 135.)

Go back to doing your work. Try again.

The boy has calmed down and is ready to get back to work.

The boy finished his work, so now he can play.

Because he kept trying, even when the work was hard, the boy completed his task.

HINT   Use this same skill when you are doing something difficult at home, or when you are learning a new skill. If you keep trying, even when the task is hard, it makes you feel good when you finally complete the task.

More Great Books You'll Want to Read!

Navigating the Social World by Jeanette McAfee, M.D. Foreword by Dr. Tony Attwood

This book has received the highest citation by the Library Journal as "essential in all collections" because of its unique focus on teaching the critical social skills autistic children lack. Ground-breaking because this books creates a bridge between theory and practice, Navigating tops the charts on the internet in sales on autism/Aspeger's. **$49.95**

Teaching Asperger's Students Social Skills Through Acting
by Amelia Davies Foreword by Jeanette McAfee, M.D.

To teach "the fine art of fitting in," Amelia Davies instructs anyone who has a sense of humor and the desire to give their kids "a healthy dose of self-esteem" how to utilize the dramatic arts to build social skills. Exercises, practical advice and scripts are provided. **$19.95**

Taking Care Of Myself   by Mary Wrobel

This book offers an unique combination of social stories and easy-to-understand activities which reduce the fear and/or confusion surrounding hygiene, puberty and personal care for young people with autism. **$24.95**

The New Social Story Book - Illustrated Edition
by Carol Gray

An illustrated version of Carol Gray's "Social Stories" concept, the book shows the child a visual represetation of the story. Parents are given a vital tool to teaching skills, such as learning to share, smile, listen, play with animals, wash hands, take showers, eat spaghetti, set the table, give gifts, make a bed and clean a room, vacuum, do homework, ride in a car, get a haircut, buy shoes, and a myriad of other important skills for the child on the autism spectrum. **$34.95**

To order these or any of our wide variety of resources, log onto our website at:

www.FutureHorizons-autism.com
or call us at: 800-489-0727

Feel free to call us with your questions or comments